This book is exactly what we young mamas need. It's not too wordy or lengthy and yet I walk away from the day's reading thinking about and pondering the jewels I just read. I can't help but think of Titus 2:3-5 where scripture exhorts older women to "Teach what is good" to the younger women. We need more of this in our churches today. Your book shows us how to take Scripture and apply it to our lives . . . to make it personal in our own homes. We should dwell on His Word and try to see what God is teaching us and not worry about what others think but what He thinks. It's only His opinion that really matters. It's very practical and relatable. And I'd like to think my home is now more fun for my kiddos (and my husband) thanks to reading your book!

— *Crystal S.*

This devotional journal has blessed me immensely, and I know it will bless others. The scriptures and wisdom are essential for young mothers. I also find it very relatable to both young mothers who work and those who are full time moms. This devotional book has especially been a blessing to me in this season. I am looking forward to buying copies for all the young mothers that I know.

— *Katie L.*

Reading this devotional has blessed me as I see Dea in a new way—as a wise woman who is sharing her years of mothering. It's a precious, intimate, funny book that readers will find encouraging, simple, and God-centered. Not to be looked at as a to-do, but to refresh you!!

— *Kathy R.*

I read through this devotional and took something away each day to not only help me as a mother but grow as a godly woman. I thoroughly enjoyed this book and will read it again and again.

— *Dee Dee L.*

This devotional journal brings life-giving nuggets of encouragement in bite size pieces just right for me as a busy mom and entrepreneur. This book helps re-center me on what is really important. Dea has such diverse life experiences from being a mother of eight, pastor's wife, church planter, entrepreneur, businesswoman, and grandmother that she has wisdom for the diverse needs of women. I would definitely recommend this for my girlfriends. Great job, Dea. I loved it.

— *Ashley O.*

An Ox in Your Kitchen

An Ox in Your Kitchen

A Devotional Journal for Young Mothers

Dea Irby

Little BIG Publishing
Durham, NC

All rights reserved. No part of this publication may be reproduced, distributed, or transmitted in any form or by any means, including photocopying, recording, or other electronic or mechanical methods, without the prior written permission of the publisher, except in the case of brief quotations embodied in critical reviews and certain other noncommercial uses permitted by copyright law. Permission requests should be sent to littlebigpublishing@gmail.com.

First Edition: April 2021

Printed in the United States of America
ISBN: 9781648589980

THE HOLY BIBLE, NEW INTERNATIONAL VERSION® Copyright © 1973, 1978, 1984, 2011 by Biblica, Inc.® Used by permission. All rights reserved worldwide.

Author headshot: River West

Little BIG Publishing
Durham, North Carolina

To my children, my spiritual spurs,
who gave me the privilege of
experiencing motherhood and taught me
to see God's grace and mercy.

I love you.

Table of Contents

Preface 1
DAY 1 — *An Ox in Your Kitchen* 3
DAY 2 — *Known by Name* 7
DAY 3 — *Actions, Not Words* 11
DAY 4 — *All My Arrows* 15
DAY 5 — *An Audience of One* 19
DAY 6 — *A Quiet Life* 23
DAY 7 — *Authentic Singing* 27
DAY 8 — *Don't Skip Step One* 31
DAY 9 — *For Powerful Results* 35
DAY 10 — *Frog-Looking Eyes* 39
DAY 11 — *Bubbles* 43
DAY 12 — *Not Begging* 47
DAY 13 — *God Can't Be Everywhere* 51
DAY 14 — *Life-itosis* 55
DAY 15 — *Mental Multitasking* 59
DAY 16 — *Mirror, Mirror* 63
DAY 17 — *Skipping* 67
DAY 18 — *Keep Silent* 71
DAY 19 — *My To-Do List* 75
DAY 20 — *Growing in Knowledge* 79
DAY 21 — *Like a Baby* 83
DAY 22 — *The Big Reveal* 87
Day 23 — *Thermostat* 91
DAY 24 — *Even the Crevices* 95
DAY 25 — *The Tooth Will Set You Free* 99
DAY 26 — *Copy Cats* 103
DAY 27 — *Witnesses* 107
DAY 28 — *Tale of Two Women* 111
DAY 29 — *How Much Longer, Mama?* 115
DAY 30 — *Inexpressible and Glorious Joy* 119
DAY 31 — *You Will Abound* 123
And a Story — *Golden Christmas Bells* 127
Scripture References 131

Preface

BEING A MOTHER IS A HIGH calling. Every woman who has been called to motherhood has her own story, her own experiences with God. I have birthed and raised eight children. In this devotional journal, I share some of my encounters with the Word and insights from the Holy Spirit. These stories and lessons are not meant to be the end-all answers. Prayerfully, they are the beginning point for you to jump into your own encounters and insights.

Enjoy, dig in, and may your adventure be blessed as you write your story. Tip: You may want to use an additional journal for even more thoughts. You may also want to read through this more than once. You will be surprised at the new perspectives you get on the second reading, and third, and . . . .

"And this is my prayer: that your love may abound more and more in knowledge and depth of insight, so that you may be able to discern what is best and may be pure and blameless for the day of Christ, filled with the fruit of righteousness that comes through Jesus Christ —to the glory and praise of God."
— Philippians 1:9-11

DAY 1

An Ox in Your Kitchen

"Where no oxen are, the manger is clean, but much increase comes by the strength of the ox."

Proverbs 14:4

THE FIRST TIME I READ THIS verse and really noticed it, I had four children all under age six. What does this have to do with oxen? I had a seemingly unrealistic goal of an immaculate home. I had tried telling myself that I needed the house "company clean" because at any time "company" might drop by to visit the pastor's family. After realizing that I was living to please others, I made my desire more spiritual by thinking that at any time Jesus might return.

I wanted to be ready for His company.

This goal, as honorable as it may have been, was causing me to resent the little mess-makers who lived in our house. As soon as one room was clean, four others were a wreck again. Do you ever feel like saying to gift-givers, "Please don't give my kids toys that have more than two parts!?"

I reread Proverbs 14:4 and discovered the answer. If I had no oxen, I could reach my goal of a clean house without fear of imminent destruction! But I would be trading away the increase of joy and laughter and a child's eye view of life that God had been using to teach me and give me strength.

Four more children came over the next 17 years. My house was never really "company clean." There is a place for daily instruction in responsibilities. My older children could and did help maintain a semblance of order in our home, some with more concern than others. I prayed to focus on joy and fun more than cleanliness.

Clean the house for "organized chaos." Don't worry about the oxen in the kitchen! This too shall pass.

Dear Lord, please give me perspective that appreciates Your Gifts to me and reminds me of the quote: "Hush away cobwebs, dust go to sleep. I'm rocking my baby and babies don't keep." Amen.

Journal Prompts

What blessings do I have because of my oxen?

What is my level of "organized chaos?"

How does this verse relate to my life?

DAY 2

Known by Name

*"He determines the number of the stars
and calls them each by name."*

Psalm 147:4

Raising eight children, I often found myself going through all the names before I got to "oh, you know who you are!" Now, with eighteen and counting grandchildren, I get even more tongue-twisted.

I can't imagine God being able to call every star by name! As far as I know, no one can even count them all. Yet God has given each one a name. I'm in awe.

If God knows a star by name, how much more does He know each of His children by name?

There is power in being known by your name. It acknowledges your own specific identity. You aren't invisible. You hold a place in the world. Not only does God know your name, He knows how many hairs you have on your head. You are known by the Creator of the universe who can name all the stars. And so am I.

After mentioning the heavens, the moon, and the stars, the Psalmist asks: "[W]hat is mankind that you are mindful of them, human beings that you care for them?" (Psalm 8:4). Then he answers his own question. "You have made them a little lower than the angels and crowned them with glory and honor" (Psalm 8:5). What an answer!

Dear Lord, it is reassuring that you know me–and each of us–by name. Help me to remember how much you love me. Amen.

Journal Prompts

What does my name mean and why was I given it?

How did I choose the name(s) for my child(ren) and why?

When I think about God naming all the stars, I realize . . .

DAY 3

Actions, Not Words

*"Like one who takes away a garment on a cold day,
or like vinegar poured on soda,
is one who sings songs to a heavy heart."*

Proverbs 25:20

Every parent who has had a child do a science project has likely made the volcano filled with baking soda and poured vinegar into it for the effective eruption. I know I did. (If your child isn't old enough yet, remember this for the future!) It is quite impressive. Adding red food coloring adds a dramatic touch. This seems to be a modern concept and yet we find it mentioned in Proverbs. Did they do science experiments back then?

I thought of this verse when I had the opportunity to do relief work through my company for a homeowner whose house was flooded during a hurricane. The water level was above her kitchen counters. Mold was growing up the walls and on all the water-logged contents. We had to remove furniture, decor, personal belongings, and gut the kitchen. We busted out the drywall from the floor to above the water line.

The owner was there and appreciated our donated

efforts. It would have been easy to offer trite "comforting" words like "Everything happens for a reason." or "All things work together for good." That's not what we did. She was operating in an adrenaline stupor and needed actions not words. I have never experienced her grief or loss, and my words would have been empty. My actions said more.

The vision of the foaming, fizzing volcano helps me remember that words, albeit well-meaning, are ineffective when the person has a heavy heart. A burdened or grieving person can use a hug or even a smile without any words. A hug or smile or just being present communicates enough. Words aren't necessary.

Dear Lord, thank you for this instruction on how to minister to burdened people. Give me compassion and close my lips. Amen.

Journal Prompts

How can I offer my child the freedom to express a heavy heart?

How can I make sure that I don't just offer words of comfort to my child but that I offer action comfort?

What are the signs that my child needs actions and not words?

DAY 4

All My Arrows

*"Like arrows in the hands of a warrior
are sons born in one's youth.
Blessed is the man whose quiver is full of them."*

Psalm 127:4-5a

First, let me say that everyone's quiver is a different size. God determines the capacity. Maybe your quiver is made for one, maybe twelve! With my eight children, I often quote this verse and then add, "And I'm quiverful!" We had no clue what size our quiver was when we married. Our children came in "batches." First, we had a daughter, then two sons, and then another daughter. "That's nice," I thought, "we now have our even family." Life progressed, the children grew, and the last was about to start school (YAY!).

For the first time in a decade, I felt like I could get dressed in the morning and still be somewhat presentable that evening. The scent of ammonia had faded. Are you there yet? (A side note: Disposable diapers are biblical: "He who Pampers his slave from childhood will in the end find him to be a son." (Proverbs 29:21).)

I thought my quiver was full. Nope. The Lord saw fit

to bless us with another son. And another son. And another son (affectionately referred to as The Three Musketeers). Let's see, isn't seven the biblical number of completion, the perfect number? Is my quiver full now? Nope. Eight years later, on number six's 10th birthday, when I was 45, a precious daughter was added.

In case you've lost count, that's three decades of having babies. Each arrow that was added stretched my quiver and increased our blessings. I don't want to think of life without any one of them.

I have prayed three things for each of them: 1) that they would love God with a whole heart; 2) that they would do what is right in His sight; and 3) that they would serve God in a great and mighty way.

Dear Lord, hear my prayers for my arrows and help me be a steadfast archer who glorifies You. Amen.

Journal Prompts

Am I open to God deciding the size of my quiver? Why or why not?

How can I pray for each arrow?

What am I doing to prepare my arrow(s) to be able to fly straight to hit the target God has planned?

DAY 5

An Audience of One

". . . We must obey God rather than men!"
Acts 5:29

IN A THEATER PRODUCTION, PROFESSIONAL ACTORS are on stage to perform for expectant onlookers with a stage manager perhaps off stage encouraging their efforts. In the ministry, "professional Christians" (also known as church staff and their families) are often on stage to perform for the congregation with God in the wings encouraging. Will there be a standing ovation? Will the reviews be good or bad?

This fear of the reviews was very strong as we moved to our new church. At that time, we had four children, ages two, four, six and eight. To welcome the new pastor and his family, the church had prepared a reception. Our very gregarious four-year-old son was flitting around meeting and greeting. In his excitement, he spilled his red punch. Very quietly, but with fervor, he determined to clean it up. A mother should be so proud . . . if he had not grabbed someone's WHITE crocheted shawl! Aaaarrrggghhh! What will people think?

It was within the first few Sundays that our two-year-old

daughter was found at church without her shoes on.

Oh, what will people think of the preacher's family whose children are so disrespectful and uncouth? I was put in my place when I confronted the barefoot culprit. (Remember, she is two.) She innocently looked up at me and said, "But Mommy, Moses took his shoes off on holy ground!"

You do not have to be a preacher's wife to feel pressure to perform. As a young mother, it is easy to think you have to parent correctly because everyone is watching. If your child misbehaves, it must be that you are not doing your job.

Oh, to have the perspective of my two-year-old! Only God's review matters. Only God sits in the audience. The Holy Spirit is in the wings prompting, and Jesus is empowering us to act out God's script for our lives. We should live before an audience of ONE.

Dear Lord, forgive me for living for the approval of humankind and not for You. Amen.

Journal Prompts

How do I let the opinions of others affect me?

What can I do to ensure I live before an audience of one?

When I hear this quote: "What other people think of me is none of my business," I think . . .

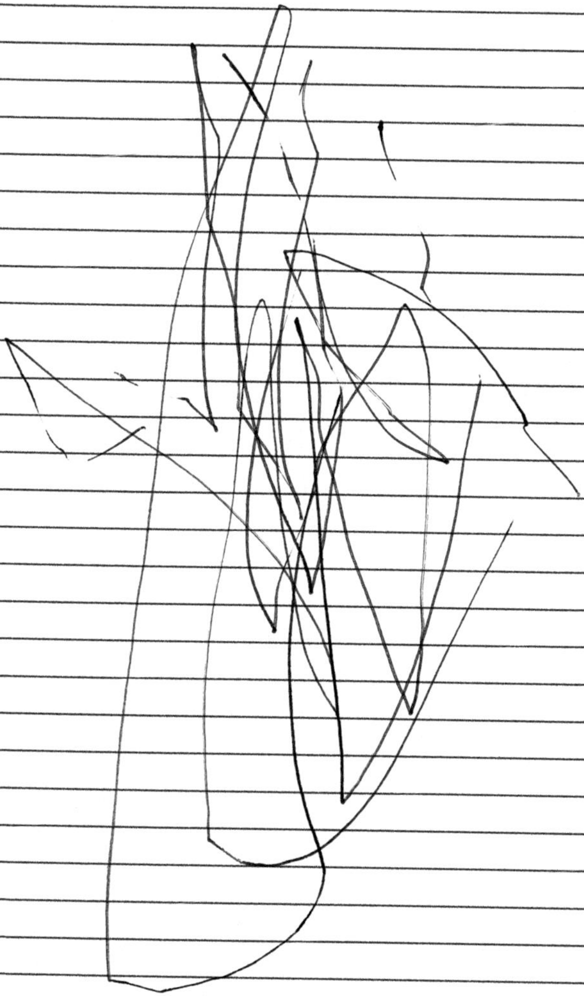

DAY 6

A Quiet Life

*"and to make it your ambition
to lead a quiet life..."*

I Thessalonians 4:11a

"Yeah, right." The first time this verse jumped out at me was when I had five children. God was telling me to have an ambition of living a quiet life? There was nothing about my life that was quiet. Yet, God was directing me to this verse. How was this possible?

Then I found another verse: "Rather, it should be that of your inner self, the unfading beauty of a gentle and quiet spirit, which is of great worth in God's sight..." (I Peter 3:4). God wasn't talking about my life around me that I couldn't control, He was directing me to my own life inside of me.

Also, Psalm 23:2b says: "He leads me beside quiet waters." Here, of course, David is referring to God as his Shepherd. A Good Shepherd leads the sheep to water, an essential need. It must be quiet water or the skittish sheep will not rest. I realized that my quiet heart would provide a "resting place" for my flock.

Another verse that impressed me with the importance

of a quiet heart is Proverbs 17:1: "Better a dry crust with peace and quiet than a house full of feasting, with strife." A home with peace and quiet of heart is more desirable than riches.

I do appreciate that I Thessalonians 4:11a says to "make it your ambition." I understand that a quiet heart is not always going to be a reality. A quiet heart is what I should strive for. Just as I am to provide a quiet heart for my flock, God provides quietness for me to rest. With the ambition of resting with my Shepherd to provide rest for my flock, I began finding little pockets of time to stop and meditate on a verse for the day. My portable prayer room, aka the family van, was a common quiet time space to use while waiting for pickup or after drop off. The more I looked for opportunities to quiet my heart, the more I found. The stronger the ambition, the better the goal was reached.

Dear Lord, strengthen my ambition to have a quiet life and show me ways to sit by Your quiet waters to rest. Amen.

Journal Prompts

My favorite place/time to have a quiet rest with my Shepherd is . . .

What is my ambition for my life?

What can I do to develop a quiet life?

DAY 7

Authentic Singing

"Keep your tongue from . . . speaking deceit."
Psalm 34:13

We really had only one major rule in our house:

Do Not Lie!

If you think you will get in trouble for doing something, you probably will. But, if you lie to get out of it, you double your trouble! At our house, authenticity is highly regarded in words and actions. This, of course, extends outside the house.

When one of our sons was about three, we were singing praise songs in church. He loved to sing (he is now in music ministry) and always joined in. We were standing and singing "I Exalt Thee," and I noticed that he was sitting, arms crossed with a scowl on his face. I chastised him, "Stand up! Sing, Seth!"

He responded, "No!"

I ordered, "Yes!"

Then, in his defense, he said, "But I'm not exhausted!"

"Ohhh!"

I had totally missed his authenticity and misinterpreted his actions. What appeared to be rebellion on the outside was genuine obedience on the inside.

That experience came to mind the other day in church when we were singing about kneeling before the Lord. Was I going to be authentic? I had a mental struggle going on: *How can I sing this standing up? Should I kneel? What would people think? It shouldn't matter what people think! Isn't it just a matter of my heart kneeling before God anyway? Or was that a lie of the enemy to make me compromise what God may be telling me? I want my words to be truthful, Lord.*

My brain hurt, so I decided that I should quietly, albeit, on the front row, kneel. I did. In the future, I may or may not physically kneel every time we sing about kneeling, but my heart will kneel and my lips will sing in truth.

Dear Lord, help me to be so involved in the words that I sing that I sing in truth and authenticity. Amen.

Journal Prompts

When have I misinterpreted the actions of my child?

Are my words in line with my heart?

How important to me is authenticity?

DAY 8

Don't Skip Step One

"Submit therefore to God, resist the devil and he will flee from you."

James 4:7

ARE YOU A COOK OR A baker? Have you made your first Thanksgiving meal for a crowd? A video submitted on television's *America's Funniest Home Videos* was about a young wife proudly serving her first turkey at a family gathering. It looked great, but she had skipped step one: take the giblet packet out of the turkey cavity. Well, in her defense, she thought it was prepared stuffing. No real harm was done. But sometimes it is quite detrimental to skip step one.

I was struggling with a mental temptation, mumbling arguments in my mind until I began to counsel myself: "Resist the devil, and he will flee from you. Resist the devil, and he will flee from you." No matter how sincerely and earnestly I chastised myself, I was getting no relief.

"Where is that verse?" I asked. I looked through my concordance until I found the James 4:7 reference. I turned to it and read, "Submit therefore to God . . ."

Whoa! So that was my problem. I left out the empowering part of the verse. Step One!

Then I saw a vision of myself as a little lamb. How often I run to the edge of the pasture and yell at the wolf to go away when I should be hiding behind the Shepherd and asking Him to take care of the wolf. As Peter wrote: "For you were continually straying like sheep, but now you have returned to the Shepherd and Guardian of your souls" (I Peter 2:25).

Don't skip step one—submit to God!

In the challenges of parenting, it is easy to miss step one: plugging into the power. God wants us to rely on Him for wisdom and strength. And you know there are many times during the day when those are needed.

Dear Lord, help me to submit to you to be empowered so I may overcome temptation. Amen.

Journal Prompts

How do I plug into God?

What story do I have about skipping step one?

When have I found power in step one to face challenges?

DAY 9

For Powerful Results...

*"But you will receive power when
the Holy Spirit has come upon you."*

Acts 1:8a

My daughter and her family served on the mission field in Brazil for nine years, and I was often the beneficiary of their cultural experience. For my tearoom, I even created a popular dish based on a Brazilian staple. I called it The Frango Surprise. A soft, hidden cream cheese, shredded chicken, and mozzarella mixture was found with each bite into the flaky pastry.

Also, when I visited my daughter, I got to enjoy some enviable (and quite affordable) pampering customs—full body massages, manicures, and pedicures.

I purchased a wonderful hand and foot lotion that helps dry skin. I applied a bit of that lotion to my hands and rubbed it in. It felt moist as I began to spread the cream, but as I continued wringing my hands, the cream soon began to slough off dry skin. After washing my hands, I applied a moisturizing lotion.

Oh, that felt supreme! I hadn't realized how rough my hands were until they weren't.

I pondered this process. If I had not applied the lotion but had vigorously rubbed my hands together, wringing them with diligence, I would not have achieved the same result. It would have been futile. No matter how sincere I was, the results would not be the same as when I was using the lotion.

Then I likened this process to the work of the Holy Spirit. How often in my Christian walk have I diligently tried to work off the dead skin of sin or sinful habits in my life! Without applying the "lotion" of the Holy Spirit, I am powerless. Oh, maybe I will feel better because I worked hard at change, but it is still futile.

In parenting, we can go through all the motions of discipline and training, but grace through the Holy Spirit needs to be applied. For mighty results, apply the power of the Holy Spirit to your thoughts and actions.

Dear Lord, help me not to act in my own strength but to submit to the work of the Holy Spirit. Amen.

Journal Prompts

How can I apply the Holy Spirit in my parenting?

What story do I have of not applying the Holy Spirit?

What actions am I taking in my own strength?

DAY 10

Frog-Looking Eyes

*"When I was a child, I talked like a child,
I thought like a child, I reasoned like a child."*

I Corinthians 13:11a

"Mom, why does God hate frog-looking eyes?" My five-year-old daughter stood before me with a sincere but worried look.

"Why would you think God hates frog-looking eyes?" I asked.

She began to sing from Proverbs 6: "There are six things, even seven that the Lord hates, things He cannot stand, Frog looking eyes . . ."

"Oh no, honey," I stopped her, "that is supposed to be 'proud-looking eyes.'" She was relieved.

Another story of a child's misunderstanding: my middle-school son chose a pottery coffee cup from the shelf, and I commented that it reminded me of him. I don't remember if I told him that it was because the cup was so unique and creative but that was my reasoning.

Years later, he recounted our conversation and told me what he "heard," which was extremely different from my intended creative and unique message. He thought it reminded me of him because it was squatty and fat. His self-image was damaged for years.

As parents, we do the best that we can, but our charges still misunderstand our intentions. Communication is the best solution. First, listen to them. What did they hear us say? What did they understand us to say? Get down on the floor, look them in the eye, and intentionally listen. The other side of the formula is carefully taking time to talk with them. Choose words that they understand or explain new vocabulary.

We are told in scripture that "Foolishness is bound up in the heart of a child" (Proverbs 22:15). They talk, think, and reason like children. They sometimes will misunderstand the meaning of what we have said to them. Listen for the message they receive and make sure they haven't heard "frog-looking eyes."

Dear Lord, open my ears to hear my children and guard my mouth to speak clearly and truthfully. Amen.

Journal Prompts

What questions can I ask my child(ren) to insure clarity?

Record a story of your child(ren)'s misunderstanding.

How can I be sure to communicate more clearly?

DAY 11

Bubbles

*"A man's own folly ruins his life,
yet his heart rages against the LORD."*

Proverbs 19:3

She yelled, "I don't want bubbles!" My two-year old feverishly swished the water to get rid of the bubbles in her bath. The harder she worked to get rid of them, the more she created. What a picture of the hedonic paradox! The harder someone seeks after happiness, the less it is found.

She didn't know the rules about bubbles or follow the rules about bubbles. By her very actions, she was "ruining her life." She was angry at the water. Maybe she wasn't raging against the LORD, but her situation was someone else's fault.

I think of this picture when I see people doing things to their own detriment and then blaming others for the results. Personal responsibility is not in fashion today, being a victim is. If you can't get a promotion, it is the boss's fault. If you aren't doing well in school, it is the teacher's fault. If you lose a game, it's because . . . (too many options to fill in there!).

Living a life that is not as God intended and then blaming God for the results is like using water instead of gasoline for your car and then yelling at the car maker when it doesn't run. God is our manufacturer and has an owner's manual, the Bible. If we foolishly ignore God's rules and ruin our lives, we shouldn't rage against God for the results.

When my life "bubbles up," I need to stop and see if I'm "swishing the water." I shouldn't rage against God if I am the one who has stepped out of His will.

Dear Lord, thank You for Your patience when I swish my life and Your guidance to show me my folly. Amen.

Journal Prompts

In what ways am I splashing water to get rid of the bubbles?

How am I encouraging my child(ren) to accept the responsibility of his/her actions and not blame others?

This is my prayer . . .

DAY 12

Not Begging

*"I was young and now I am old,
yet I have never seen the righteous forsaken
or their children begging bread."*

Psalm 37:25

Yes, I have lived a few years. Enough years that I've read this verse multiple times. This verse was always comforting to know, especially when we were stretching dollars to feed our many young mouths.

Today, for the first time, I saw this verse differently. The children of the righteous are not begging for bread because God is providing. Yes—but also they are not begging because the righteous have taught their children to work. There is a connected verse that states: "The one who is unwilling to work shall not eat" (II Thessalonians 3:10). If someone is capable of working, not willing to work, and is expecting a handout, they shall not eat. Emphasis on capable.

A sense of relief has come over me! This means I was not a cruel parent to have my children do a paper route with me. Every weekday we went to the *Atlanta Journal Constitution* and assembled our papers and ran our route. The youngest was strapped in on the very back seat (often throwing up from the ride!) In the middle of the night, with the help of one of the older children, we delivered the weekend papers.

Proverbs 16:26 states: "The appetite of laborers works for them; their hunger drives them on." Nothing like hunger to motivate a person to work! The righteous teach their children that work is a good thing, and God blesses them with bread. God also can and does bless children "just because." But they are never seen begging.

Dear Lord, remind me of the value of work. Help me to see your gracious hand of provision but never sit back and expect it. Amen.

Journal Prompts

What am I teaching my child(ren) about work?

How can I teach a balance of dependence on God's grace and working?

My view of work has been . . .

DAY 13

God Can't Be Everywhere

"Am I a God who is near," declares the Lord,
"And not a God far off?"
Jeremiah 23:23

When I was a young mother, a popular slogan was seen plastered on various pieces of decor—"God can't be everywhere. That's why He made Mothers." This perspective was promoting the importance of being a mom. True, moms are valuable. Since I was "only a stay-at-home mom," it was encouraging to see my elevated position as God's helper.

A better version would state: "Moms can't be everywhere, that's why they need God." Two instances come to mind when I experienced this truth.

The first experience happened when I was pregnant with my third child. My two young children were playing nicely so I was taking a moment to rest. My moment was brief. I heard frantic "help, help" cries from the hallway. I rolled off the couch and slowly righted myself to walk around the corner. I found my two-year old, hanging from the outside of the banister at the top of the stairs with his arms hung between the rails. Praise God, He was there holding my son until I could rescue him.

The second experience that comes to mind is when my sons were two and four, the two-year-old was convinced he was Superman. He would create capes with towels, sheets, big shirts or anything he could. He would race down the stairs like he was flying. His "wiser, older brother" would encourage him in this. I learned, years after the fact that the older, wiser brother had almost convinced him to fly out the second floor window. God was there, Praise Jesus. My son decided not to try it.

Dear Lord, thank you for being everywhere. Never let me forget how much I need you every day in every way. Amen.

Journal Prompts

How have I seen God at work in my life protecting my child(ren)?

What can I tell God to express my dependence on His ever watchful eye?

Has my perspective changed? If so, how?

DAY 14

Life-itosis

*"Their robes were not scorched,
and there was no smell of fire on them."*

Daniel 3:27c

WHAT'S THAT SMELL? AS A MOM, we discover many curious smells in the house—a forgotten diaper, a messy, discarded pair of underwear, or a half-eaten apple. Smells are everywhere. Smells tell a story.

Halitosis is a condition commonly referred to as bad breath. Years ago, a television commercial was created that warned about "house-itosis" and offered cures. I began thinking about smells in the Bible. A soothing aroma is mentioned in the sacrificial instructions over and over: "But you shall present a burnt offering, an offering by fire, as a soothing aroma to the LORD" (Numbers 29:6). The Bible also tells us that our prayers are a sweet aroma to God.

An instance of a not so pleasant smell is in John 11:39: "Jesus said, 'Remove the stone.' Martha, the sister of the deceased, said to Him, 'Lord, by this time there will be a stench, for he has been dead four days.'"

As I thought about all these instances, the story in

Daniel came to mind. Three men were thrown into a fiery furnace. But they were joined by a fourth man. The men who threw them into the fire were burned up because the fire was so hot. Yet the three children of Israel were able to come out alive and well and "smelling like a rose," so to speak.

Christians are instructed to be in the world but not of the world. Isn't this what happened to these men? Christ joined them in the fire, and they escaped without being burned or even smelling like smoke. As I live in the world, being salt and light, my life should be a sweet aroma to God and to others. The only way this is possible is to walk with "the Fourth Man."

Smell became very important to me as I considered this analogy. There are good smells and there are bad smells. There are roses and there is poop. There is a godly aroma, and there is a worldly aroma. I desire to be a sweet aroma, roses, a godly smell.

Dear Lord, make my life a sweet aroma in your nostrils. Amen.

Journal Prompts

When do I smell bad to God?

What in my life makes me smell like smoke?

How can I offer up a sweet aroma to God?

DAY 15

Mental Multitasking

*"And forgive us our debts,
as we also have forgiven our debtors."*
Matthew 6:12

MULTITASKING IS A TERM CREATED TO describe the rapid actions of computers that *seem* to be happening at the same time. According to science, it is not possible for people. In spite of the science, I consider myself a master at multitasking, of being a jill-of-all-trades!

I am sure you can relate. Motherhood calls for it. I've nursed a baby while cooking and talking on the phone and helping a child do homework. I've worked on my computer while watching a football game and listening to music. I know you are probably able to do the same. We must if we are going to live up to that ode to a capable wife in Proverbs 31:10-31!

This "condition" causes a problem sometimes in church. Does this ever happen to you? I'm sitting or standing there participating, yet my mind is making a list of people to talk with after service or planning what to do for dinner. Typically, I get away with this (from my perspective only), but one Sunday God spoke loud and clear.

My mind had wandered off to my business. I needed to expand my shelving and storage at my tearoom. I didn't have any money in my budget for it. Who would be able to help me if I bought the supplies? Oh, I know. Mr. "Unidentified." He is a builder and fully capable. And, I continued to reason, after what happened with him and my family, he owes us. He should do this for free.

As I was thinking these thoughts, I was standing reciting the Lord's Prayer and we came to the portion "and forgive us our debts, as we also have forgiven our debtors."

Oh, God, I am so sorry! I was struck with deep conviction. And I certainly didn't want God to forgive me as I was (actually wasn't) forgiving Mr. "Unidentified." I praise God that He disciplines me and purifies my heart!

Dear Lord, reveal to me my sinful un-forgiveness and help me to love with your love. Amen.

Journal Prompts

Whom do I need to forgive?

How am I multitasking?

This reminds me of . . .

DAY 16

Mirror, Mirror

"Finally, brethren, whatever is true, whatever is honorable, whatever is right, whatever is pure, whatever is lovely, whatever is of good repute, if there is any excellence and if anything worthy of praise, dwell on these things."

Philippians 4:8

WHAT IS THE TAPE PLAYING IN your mind—those thoughts that continually run through your brain in the background that create your perspective and mood?

I have a story about my tape. "I need a mirror in the shower so I can see myself when I shave," my husband had said many times. I finally remembered. Standing in the middle of the tub, I calculated various placements. After about 15 minutes, I committed to THE PERFECT SPOT. The anchor tapes grabbed the fiberglass as I pressed the mirror. No changing now. Fully committed. My husband would be happy. I felt a sense of pride.

I stepped out of the tub and resumed my daily chores of taking care of my babies. My steps were lighter. A tape began playing in my head. "Good job, you saw a need and filled it, you are such a great wife." I waited with anticipation for my husband to discover his surprise. And waited. And waited.

After a couple of days, I asked, "Did you see the mirror I put in the shower?"

"Yeah, it's too low," he answered. He finished his breakfast and was gone for the day.

The tape in my head rewound with a screech like an old reel-to-reel recorder and started playing a new message. "You can't get anything right. Boy, you blew that."

At that time, I was studying a book by Larry Crabb that talked about changing the tapes in our minds. Reprogram them. I needed to remember that "What other people think of me is none of my business!" I began focusing on remembering God loves me no matter what and being thankful for all the true, honorable, right, pure, and lovely things around me.

It wasn't right for me to think that someone else could make or break my value. My value was in Jesus Christ—as it always will be—no matter what others say or do. I changed the tape playing in my mind. MY mirror was in the perfect spot, seeing myself as God sees me.

Dear Lord, help me see my value in you and focus on things that are true, honorable, right, pure, lovely, and of good repute. Amen.

Journal Prompts

What is the tape I hear playing in my head?

What can I focus on that plays a better tape?

*When have I played the wrong tape
and what was the result?*

DAY 17

Skipping

"In Him and through faith in Him, we may approach God with freedom and confidence."

Ephesians 3:12

CHILDREN CAN BE SO FULL OF joy. They easily express their emotions. They are a reminder of the freedom in innocence. They can skip through their days.

I was finishing my cup of coffee before entering worship. A Sunday-best-dressed girl of about four skipped by me full of joy. She skipped so freely and joyously. Was it a newfound skill? Was it her youthfulness? I thought, *"When did I stop skipping? When does anyone stop skipping? Why do we stop?"*

How wonderful to be a child, so free to skip with confidence. Maybe it was because I was in the church building, but I envisioned myself being that joyful in the presence of God, in His throne room, without any cares about on-lookers. Oh, to relish in the glory of being with Abba Daddy.

This carefree little girl's skipping reminded me of a word picture I had years earlier. The message was "Crashing through the throne room doors, crying

'Abba Daddy,' jumping in His loving arms, and whispering 'I love You.'"

I want to be that free and confident always.

Often when I pray, I see myself running to my Heavenly Father and climbing into His lap. Around us sparkles the gold and glitter of magnificence. The air is pure and clear. Light bounces off the floors and columns. He welcomes me there. I can approach Abba Daddy with freedom and confidence. I am convinced I should skip more—if not with my body at least with my spirit.

What a challenge to think about skipping physically! Maybe I'll go outside right now and do that. Want to join me? What's good for the body is good for the soul, right?

Dear Lord, fill me with such joy that I overflow into a skip and approach you with freedom and confidence. Amen.

Journal Prompts

The last time I skipped was . . . because . . .

This picture of joy reminds me of . . .

When I think of God on His throne, I see . . .

DAY 18

Keep Silent

"Even a fool is thought wise if he keeps silent, and discerning if he holds his tongue."
Proverbs 17:28

WHEN YOU ARE ON MOMMY PATROL, it seems like adult conversations are few and far between. I was enjoying a rare night out with adults. My day-to-day conversations were with toddlers to teens, so this evening was a special treat. Our table discussions went deep and wide without an interruption. How refreshing. I listened and contributed what I could. I was a bit out of practice.

Then we got into the realm of science and travel and that led into time zones. My curious mind was triggered, and I piped in with a comment about 24 time zones. Silence fell like a shroud over our table, and all eyes turned to me. *What had I said wrong?* I thought. Then someone offered, "Well, you would think there were only 24, but actually there are several more when you consider the International Dateline for example."

The memory of this conversation comes up periodically. I so wanted to have an adult conversation that I blurted out whatever words I could find. Yes, the verse for today is so true. I could have gone all night and not said anything, just listened, and perhaps been thought wise, but I did speak.

I learned a few important lessons from this experience. One, think before I speak. Considering our widespread family and all of our travels even back then, if I had stopped to think before I said anything, I probably would have known a better answer. But, what if I didn't? Maybe I didn't know what I didn't know. This challenges me to have grace for others. I should not be critical of people who ask questions with obvious answers. They don't know what they don't know, either. Or maybe they just haven't thought it through.

Perhaps I was experiencing the effect of my "sleep-deprived mom brain." This condition goes with the job sometimes. I should know to have patience and grace for questions, especially from moms with small children.

Dear Lord, help me be silent when I should and always be gracious to others. Amen.

Journal Prompts

When is a time I should have kept silent?

How can I show grace to myself and others when the conversation is off track?

What tempts me to NOT hold my tongue?

DAY 19

My To-Do List

"For we are His workmanship, created in Christ Jesus for good works, which God prepared beforehand so that we would walk in them."

Ephesians 2:10

"A woman can only do so much!" "A mom of littles can only do so much!" "There just aren't enough hours in the day (or night) to get it all done." Have you ever felt this frustration?

When I am caught up in the whirlwind, I remember today's verse in Ephesians. God has prepared my works; I am to walk in them. Even Jesus did that. At the end of His life, He had not healed every sick person or preached to every person in Israel. In fact, He didn't travel more than a hundred square miles from His hometown. However, He could say at the end of His life, "It is finished." He had marked off everything on His to-do list. How?

God prepared and wrote His to-do list. Jesus was in close communication with His Father and knew what He was supposed to do. A need did not always constitute a call.

In my overflowing life, I am challenged to be still and listen for what should be on my list. Sometimes the good steals time and energy from the best.

I have worked to make it a habit to have a piece of paper handy as I start the day with my quiet time. At the top of the paper, I usually write out the verse God gives me. Then, as things come to mind, I make my to-do list. I pray over it and adjust it, if needed. Things not completed that day can always be carried over.

Dear Father, help me to walk in the works You have placed on my to-do list. Amen.

Journal Prompts

My method of getting things done is . . .

This verse makes me realize . . .

The prayer I want to say to God at the beginning of my day is . . .

DAY 20

Growing in Knowledge

"Like newborn babies, crave pure spiritual milk, so that by it you may grow up in your salvation, now that you have tasted that the Lord is good."

I Peter 2:2-3

"Mama, will this cookie hit Jesus in the head when I swallow?" my 3 year-old daughter asked. She had recently asked Jesus to come into her heart.

We may laugh at this innocence. Children don't know any better. They are still figuring out the world. I'm sure your child has come up with some jewels. Did you write them down? You will likely forget most of it.

When we first become believers, we are considered newborn babies. Maybe we have misconceptions about how it all works. We are to crave for spiritual milk and grow in our relationship with God, our knowledge of the Word, and how to live out our faith. We, too, must figure out our new world. We start where we are with a great Teacher: "He guides the humble in what is right and teaches them his way" (Psalm 25:9).

When a child speaks in ignorance, we give them grace with understanding. God, our Father, is patient and caring when we speak or act in ignorance. We can ask as the Psalmist did: "Deal with your servant according to your love and teach me your decrees" (Psalm 119:124). And He does. He teaches us the ways of His world. His hand is in all our experiences to help us grow in knowledge. "Teach me knowledge and good judgment, for I trust your commands" (Psalm 119:66). Like a child, we don't know what we don't know—until God teaches us.

Dear Lord, help me to look to You for my knowledge and understanding. Thank you that You patiently teach me. Amen.

Journal Prompts

These are some of my favorite stories about my child(ren) . . .

What has God recently taught me that I didn't know that I didn't know about Him, Jesus, the Holy Spirit, myself?

What can I do to grow in my knowledge and relationship with my Heavenly Father?

DAY 21

Like a Baby

"Surely I have composed and quieted my soul;
Like a weaned child rests against his mother,
My soul is like a weaned child within me."

Psalm 131:2

THERE IS NOTHING MORE PEACEFUL AND beautiful than a sleeping baby. I might have been up all night walking the floor with a crying baby or gone a whole day without washing my face but the stress of all that melted away with a look at my precious little one, sleeping and satiated in my arms. The drizzle of milk at the corner of an open mouth reassured me I held a satisfied baby.

My favorite position for holding my little ones was leaning back in a recliner or slightly propped up against pillows with the sleeping baby on its stomach and against my chest. My whole body felt relaxed. The rapid, shallow breathing sounded like a lullaby and had the same effect.

Babies who are dry and full can sleep through so much: siblings playing nearby, loud music, vacuum cleaners, even deafening buzzers at basketball games. How do they do that? They have all their needs met. No hunger. No worries. No fears.

Can my soul be as composed and quieted as that sleeping, satiated infant? Yes. This verse invites me to release worries and fears and trust my Heavenly Father. I can find all the nourishment I need in God's Word and through prayer. My soul is fed. I can rest contented that God is in control and holds me in His loving embrace.

Dear Lord, thank you for Your Word that feeds my soul and enables me to be composed and quieted. Help me relax in Your loving arms as a weaned, contented child. Amen.

Journal Prompts

How can I feed my soul?

My soul is composed and quieted most when . . .

I see myself relaxed in God's arms and feel . . .

DAY 22

The Big Reveal

"Thou shalt have no other gods before me."
Exodus 20:3

THE ROLE OF MOTHERHOOD IS A privilege. The role of a mother can also be overwhelming. It is not a 9 to 5 job. It doesn't come with paid vacation. The pressure to get everything done is common with all that is required. Have you been there? Do you relate?

At one point in my life, this pressure became unbearable. I found myself begging God for relief. "How am I expected to be everywhere and take care of my widespread family? How am I supposed to know what is the best school choice for my child? How am I to stretch our resources to provide for our needs? How can I possibly do all the things expected of me?" I was on the verge of a major breakdown.

Then God broke through. I had the Big Reveal that spoke to my soul. It came as a shock at first. Ready for it? Here it is: I am not God! Only God is omnipresent.

Only God is omniscient. Only God is omnipotent. God reassured me that He had things under control. I could climb up into His lap and relax in His arms.

He has the whole world in HIS hands. I should focus on being in His presence and stop thinking I'm God. A wash of relief restored me.

Being God is too big of a job, and I don't need the pressure!

Dear Lord, forgive me when I try to take over and do Your job. Help me to trust in You and relinquish my control. Amen.

Journal Prompts

I am trying to be God when I . . .

I want to turn over . . . to God and ask Him to take care of the results.

I trust God to be everywhere, to know everything, and to be able to do anything He desires. This makes me feel . . .

Day 23

Thermostat

*"A righteous man who walks in his integrity—
how blessed are his sons after him."*

Proverbs 20:7

How did my children know when I was at my wit's end? When I was on my last nerve, they could instinctively step on it. Do you find that to be true?

One day, amid chaos and pondering my situation, I thought of our thermostat. It sets the temperature. I like it higher, and my husband likes it lower. Whoever wins the thermostat war determines the temperature. There was my clue. Whoever sets the thermostat, sets the temperature—hot or cold.

This verse in the Amplified version says: "A righteous man who walks in integrity and lives life in accord with his [godly] beliefs—how blessed [happy and spiritually secure] are his children after him [who have his example to follow]." Hmm, I realize I am the emotional and spiritual thermostat that sets the emotional and spiritual temperature of the environment in my home.

Just like I know a fever means my child is sick, I know that the high temperature of the emotional atmosphere means something is wrong. When tension is in the air, I need to check my spiritual thermostat. What is it set on? Colossians 3:2 states: "Set your affection on things above, not on things on the earth." Have I taken my eyes off Jesus? Am I not living in accordance with my godly beliefs? What is the example I am setting for my children to follow?

Dear Lord, help me look at my own spiritual temperature and reset my thermostat so that Your peace will fill the air. Amen.

Journal Prompts

What is my emotional thermostat set on?

What is my spiritual thermostat set on?

This reminds me of the time . . .

DAY 24

Even the Crevices

*"You scrutinize my path and my lying down,
And are intimately acquainted with all my ways."*

Psalm 139:3

I WRAPPED THE SLIPPERY WET INFANT in the hooded towel as I raised her from the baby tub on the kitchen counter. Every little crease and crevice needed to be carefully dried. I knew every inch, rather millimeter, of my child. I was intimately acquainted with all its ways. I searched between the folds for any droplets of moisture that might remain so I could prevent a rash. I searched out of love not judgement. I wanted the best for my child.

I can't think of a better picture than how intimately acquainted God is with all my ways. He diligently searches the folds of my heart to root out any moisture of sin that can grow into a rash of disobedience. He does this because He loves me, not because He is judging me. Am I submitting to His search?

Just like my child trusts me to look for the water droplets, I want to allow God to search my heart for the droplets of sin.

As it says in Psalms 139:23-24: "Search me, God, and know my heart; test me and know my anxious thoughts. See if there is any offensive way in me and lead me in the way everlasting."

When the baby wiggles and squirms, it is hard to get to all the water droplets. When I wiggle and squirm under God's scrutiny, it is difficult for me to see my sin. God wants the best for me just as I want the best for my child.

I want to remember that God patiently dries me with His grace because He loves me.

Dear Lord, thank you for your patient scrutinizing of my heart, seeking to dry out any sin that might be there. Help me not to wiggle and squirm but to trust and submit. Amen.

Journal Prompts

My prayer for God to search my heart is . . .

I wiggle and squirm when God talks to me about . . .

A time God searched my crevices was when . . .

DAY 25

The Tooth Will Set You Free

"Anyone who listens to the Word but does not do what it says is like a man who looks at his face in a mirror and, after looking at himself, goes away and immediately forgets what he looks like."

James 1:23, 24

"Ooooo, that looks nasty," I said, pointing to one of the samples. The dentist held the card of tooth-color choices. I was ordering a crown, and he was allowing me to help select the one that would best match.

"That actually is the closest one to your teeth," he said. He held the remains of my removed tooth up to the selection.

I slid down in the leather chair a bit. *Do my teeth look that discolored?* I took a quick glance in a hanging mirror hoping to counter the fact but instead confirming it. I didn't often stare in the mirror and take note of my teeth.

I thought of the story of the prideful woman admiring her white laundry on the line, thinking hers was the most pure and bright. A sudden snowfall revealed the true color of her clothes as off-white and dull. The Truth was revealed by comparison.

The Word of God is the believer's standard, the mirror, to use for life comparisons. It is so easy to think I'm following God's teachings as long as I am not staring into the Word. My laundry looks bright as long as there isn't fresh fallen snow. My teeth are shiny white as long as I don't look in the mirror.

However, to grow more like Jesus, I need to look deeply into the Word, listen to the Word, and act on the Word. That is where the blessings are. "But the man who looks intently into the perfect law that gives freedom, and continues to do this, not forgetting what he has heard, but doing it—he will be blessed in what he does" (James 1:25).

Dear Lord, help me stare deeply into the mirror of Your Word and remember to do what I learn. Amen.

Journal Prompts

How can I make sure I spend time in the Word?

This reminds me of . . .

What do I learn about man's nature?

DAY 26

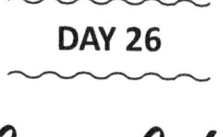

Copy Cats

"Be imitators of me, just as I also am of Christ."
I Corinthians 11:1

From the time my children were eating solid food, I began teaching table manners. Drawing on my Girl Scout days, I taught them a few jingles like: "Mable, Mable, if you're able, get your elbows off the table." They were told the salt and pepper were married and should be passed together even if someone asks for only one. Before we began eating, after our prayer, I'd remind them to put their napkins in their laps. I melodically asked, "Who has their napkin in their lap?" with a definite cadence. Everyone would raise their hands and say, "me!" enthusiastically, even the toddler.

One day I said, "da da da da da da da da?" with the same rhythm and tone. The toddler threw up her arm and said, "me." She had learned to copy her siblings without even knowing what was said. I think of this story when I see this verse. Our children are copycats, imitating our actions and reactions, even when we don't realize it. They also copy their siblings.

The important part is the "just as I also am of Christ."

First, as a mom, I want to keep my eyes on Jesus and have His attitude and take His actions. My children will imitate whatever I am doing or being. They may not even know why they are doing what they are doing. They are acting and reacting as they have seen. Just as my toddler responded without the proper words, so much is caught and not taught.

Ephesians 5:1-2 also teaches: "Therefore be imitators of God, as beloved children; and walk in love, just as Christ also loved you and gave Himself up for us, an offering and a sacrifice to God as a fragrant aroma." I am to be as a beloved child imitating God even when I might not understand it all.

Dear Lord, show me how I can be more like You so that when my child imitates me, he/she is imitating You. Amen.

Journal Prompts

This reminds me of the time . . .

I realize that I am imitating my mom when I . . .

In what ways can I be an imitator of Christ?

DAY 27

Witnesses

"But you will receive power when the Holy Spirit comes on you; and you will be my witnesses in Jerusalem, and in all Judea and Samaria, and to the ends of the earth."

Acts 1:8

OUR CHURCH WAS HAVING A TRAINING class for members to learn to share the Gospel. Emphasis was placed on "all believers are to evangelize." The course was covering phone evangelism and how to share through calling people in the phone book. (Yes, last century there were things called phonebooks with a list of names, addresses, and landline home numbers.) I had four small children at home all under seven and felt unfaithful because I did not participate. How would I find the time to be on the phone?

I totally agreed that every believer should be able to share the gospel. We are told that we should prepare for that in I Peter 3:15: "But in your hearts revere Christ as Lord. Always be prepared to give an answer to everyone who asks you to give the reason for the hope that you have. But do this with gentleness and respect." I also knew that the locations listed in Acts 1:8, Jerusalem, Judea, Samaria and then the ends of the earth, started where the listeners were and continued out to bigger areas, much like we would say city, state, nation, and world. I looked around my little Jerusalem, inside my walls. I had four little people to "evangelize," to bring up in the nurture of the Lord. I had time for this.

I look back now and see my investment in my own Jerusalem did reach the ends of the earth. All four have lived around the globe, sharing the Gospel, discipling young believers. As a mom, the Lord has put in front of you a great mission field to plow up and plant, to water and prune. Invest in the Jerusalem inside your walls. Prepare your child to use their God-given gifts and abilities. They may go around the world. They may be the one to share with the person who goes. They may have the lost from around the world on their hearts and give generously to support others who go. God has His plan in His economy, and He will work out the results. Be faithful in your Jerusalem.

Dear Lord, help me to see the value of investing the Gospel in my own Jerusalem. Help me be faithful and prepared with an answer for all their questions. Amen.

Journal Prompts

How can I serve in my Jerusalem?

The way I explain the Gospel to my child is . . .

Some of the questions I want to be prepared to answer are . . .

DAY 28

Tale of Two Women

"Let all who are simple come to my house!"
Proverbs 9:4,16

Yes, you are a mother. First, you are a woman of God. We are focusing on YOU today as we consider Proverbs 9. Reading through this passage, I found the comparison of the two women striking. Both are welcoming passersby, encouraging them to come in. Both offer food and drink. One has built her house, prepared her meat, mixed her wine, and set her table. The other is unruly, simple, knows nothing, and sits at the door. One leads to life; the other to death.

Without discernment, it is so easy to be deceived. Often the invitation sounds the same. Both women are making a call to "those who have no sense." How can we know whose voice is right?

A few observations might help. Wisdom is offering "my food and drink I have mixed." Folly is offering "stolen water and food eaten in secret." Wisdom challenges passersby to become better and "leave their simple ways." Folly only entices their senses and encourages their indulgences.

Wisdom is speaking from authority and authenticity. She has done the work and is offering resources from her own efforts. Her goal is the betterment of people. Before you accept teaching from someone, make sure he or she is walking the talk.

Folly is a fake! She did nothing to create her resources; she stole them. She is not walking her talk. Her goal is entrapment. "If it sounds too good to be true, it probably is." Folly doesn't understand that hard work builds character.

I have had entanglements with Folly. That person who gets in your life and sounds good but has ulterior motives. That person who gossips and slanders. That person who is negative about everything. At the call of the invitation, it is hard to see the fine line between Wisdom and Folly. How do I know how to respond to the invitation? I stay close to the Light. When I do that, the darkness is dispelled. The choice is made for me.

Dear Lord, make me like Wisdom who calls out to passersby and offers life. Amen.

Journal Prompts

How do I discern between Wisdom and Folly?

When have I listened to Wisdom and not Folly?

What do I see about God in this lesson? About me?

DAY 29

How Much Longer, Mama?

*"The Lord is not slow in keeping his promise,
as some understand slowness.
Instead, He is patient with you,
not wanting anyone to perish,
but everyone to come to repentance."*

II Peter 3:9

"How much longer, Mama? Are we there yet?" If you have ever taken a trip with a child, even if it is only across town, you have heard these questions. Tries a mama's patience. I often wonder if God feels the same way when we ask the same questions. Uh, NO.

God's timetable isn't my timetable. Peter is explaining to his listeners that God is waiting to fulfill His promise of the return of Christ until more people can become believers. He wants all to come to Jesus and that takes time. God is not being slow. He is being patient.

This message applies to each of us personally as well. When it seems that God is being slow to fulfill His promises to me, He is, in fact, being patient. God knows the right time for His promises to be completed.

God promises He will work all things together for my good. In the midst of the "working it out," it can seem God is taking too much time. Yet in God's wisdom, He is being patient to grow me and change me while He changes my circumstances.

God promises that His word will not return void, that it is powerful to accomplish the task. It sometimes seems that God is being slow when I've been praying for the salvation of someone and they still haven't come to believe. God is being patient, not slow. I still claim the fulfillment of His promise and learn patience myself.

God is not bound by time, a second is like a thousand years and a thousand years is like a second. He looks down on created time and sees it all. He is not ever late to the task. God fulfills His promises at the perfect time.

Dear Lord, give me wisdom to understand You work in Your time and help me trust that You are being patient and not slow. Amen.

Journal Prompts

When have I been impatient with God?

What do I need to trust God to handle in His time?

What do I learn about God from this? About me?

DAY 30

Inexpressible and Glorious Joy

*"Though you have not seen him, you love him;
and even though you do not see him now, you believe in
him and are filled with an inexpressible and glorious joy,
for you are receiving the end result of your faith,
the salvation of your souls."*
I Peter 1:8-9

Having carried your child inside, you understand how you can love someone you haven't seen. After all the birthing pains, a look into your precious newborn's face can melt you with joy. If your child is adopted, you loved him before you held him.

I am challenged by this verse to remember the inexpressible and glorious joy I felt when I first learned of God's immeasurable grace. Do I still carry that in my heart? I don't see Him in person and "out of sight, out of mind" is a temptation. Or am I just tired? How can I refresh that earlier joy?

One way to refresh this joy is to focus on the end result—as it says in today's verse—the salvation of my soul. If I truly understand the power in that statement, how can I not be filled with the inexpressible and glorious joy. When I think of what I'm being saved from—an eternity without God, a life here and now without purpose, direction, or belonging—meditating on this truth should "knock my socks off!"

Another way to refresh this joy is to share it with others. Like sharing about a great event or movie, the more you tell someone about it, the more it is re-lived in your mind and heart. You experience the thrill all over again. I'm sure God knows this is a side effect of sharing the Gospel with others. That is one reason He tells us to share with others. Then, seeing the joy spring up in the person you share with IS seeing God.

Like the multiplying of the boy's lunch that was used by Jesus to feed the thousands, the more we give away, the more we have. Share the joy. Increase the joy. Ignite the fire that came at salvation.

Dear Lord, fill my heart with the inexpressible and glorious joy that comes from You and knowing the end result of my salvation. Amen.

Journal Prompts

To me inexpressible and glorious joy feels like . . .

What brings up the most joy in my life?

What stifles my joy?

DAY 31

You Will Abound

"And God is able to bless you abundantly, so that in all things at all times, having all that you need, you will abound in every good work."

II Corinthians 9:8

God has blessed you with a child and the good work of motherhood. Can you abound in it? Let's see.

"And God is able." Sometimes we may be without all the resources we need. God is ABLE because He does have all the resources.

"To bless you abundantly." We give as we can. God gives over and above what is necessary. There is no limit to God's giving.

"So that in all things." ALL. There is not one thing that God does not include.

"At all times." ALL. There is never a time that God does not bless.

"Having all that you need." Notice, it doesn't say "all that you want." I'm sure your child has asked you for something and you, in your wisdom, knew it was not what they needed. Our Father is the same. And, again, it says ALL you need. God doesn't miss anything. Sometimes we may think He has forgotten us and is not providing something we need. God, from His perspective, knows and sees things we don't, and He has a reason for not providing right now, and maybe never.

"You will abound." A promise from God: you will more than survive; you will thrive.

"In every good work." Ephesians 2:10 tells us: "For we are God's handiwork, created in Christ Jesus to do good works, which God prepared in advance for us to do." We are made for those good works. God promises that we will abound in those works because they were tailor made for us.

God is the source to bless you in fulfilling the work of mothering. You will abound.

Dear Lord, thank you for being able to bless me abundantly in all things at all times so I may abound in raising my child.

Journal Prompts

Choose one or more of the phrases in II Corinthians 9:8 and write how you see it in your life in general and/or as a mother.

And a Story

Golden Christmas Bells

"Each of you should give what you have decided in your heart to give, not reluctantly or under compulsion, for God loves a cheerful giver."

II Corinthians 9:7

As I knocked on the back door, I admired the decorative golden bells hanging from red velvet ribbons. This was my last stop visiting each family of the church youth group where I worked. As a newlywed facing my first Christmas, I was very conscious of decorations that abounded in other homes. We didn't have a stockpile to pull from the attic or basement or even a closet. Our holiday budget was enough to cover food on the table and our seminary and college expenses.

Mrs. Horton answered the door with her usual cheery smile and welcomed me. Their tree stood in the family room and was full of handmade ornaments from her six children. A variety of gifts of all shapes, sizes, and colors spilled out from under the tree. It was a scene from a greeting card that should have given me joy and happiness. This family loved Jesus and celebrated His birth, which was normally exactly how I felt and wanted to live. That wasn't true at the moment, however.

The darkness of envy and jealousy began to cloud my heart and mind. This display was the tradition of my childhood, lavishly showering every room with decorations like God lavishly showers us with His love. How could I have a real Christmas without decorations?

After a short visit, Mrs. Horton walked me to the door.

"I just love these golden Christmas bells. They make the door look so festive!" I said. Mrs. Horton reached up and took them off the hook and said, "Here you go. Enjoy them."

I stumbled back. "Oh, no, I couldn't take these. They're your door decorations."

"You like them, right?" She put her hand on her hip. "I want to give them to you."

Was it the guilt about my envy and jealousy or the fact that I didn't think I deserved the gift that caused me to reject her offer?

Then, she said, "If you don't take these, you are denying me the gift of giving."

"What?" I said as I wrapped my scarf around my neck.

Mrs. Horton said, "In order for me to get to give with the Christmas spirit, someone has to receive." I got it. I went home with my first decoration. This experience was preparing me for many years of humbly accepting generosity.

Every year I hung the golden bells, remembering that receiving from others is one way God lavishes His love on us. The bells had their ribbons replaced a few times and have now been passed on to my daughter along with the story about blessing others by receiving.

Dear Lord, help me to be the gracious receiver of people's generosity, so I can allow them to be blessed by their giving. Amen.

Journal Prompts

When have I been the receiver of other's generosity?

When have I had the joy of giving generously?

This story reminds me of when . . .

Scripture References

Exodus 20:3 . . . . Day 22	Daniel 3:27c . . . . Day 14
Numbers 29:6 . . . . Day 14	Matthew 6:12 . . . . Day 15
Psalm 8:4, 5 . . . . Day 2	John 11:39 . . . . Day 14
Psalm 23:2b . . . . Day 6	Acts 1:8a . . . . Day 9
Psalm 25:9 . . . . Day 20	Acts 1:8a . . . . Day 27
Psalm 34:13 . . . . Day 7	Acts 5:29 . . . . Day 5
Psalm 37:25 . . . . Day 12	I Corinthians 11:1 . . . . Day 26
Psalm 119:66, 124 . . . . Day 20	I Corinthians 13:11a . . . . Day 10
Psalm 127:4-5a . . . . Day 4	II Corinthians 9:8 . . . . Day 31
Psalm 131:2 . . . . Day 21	Ephesians 2:10 . . . . Day 19
Psalm 139:3, 23, 24 . . . . Day 24	Ephesians 2:10 . . . . Day 31
Psalm 147:4 . . . . Day 2	Ephesians 3:12 . . . . Day 17
Proverbs 6 . . . . Day 10	Ephesians 5:1, 2 . . . . Day 26
Proverbs 9:4, 16 . . . . Day 28	Philippians 4:8 . . . . Day 16
Proverbs 14:4 . . . . Day 1	Colossians 3:2 . . . . Day 23
Proverbs 16:26 . . . . Day 12	I Thessalonians 4:11a . . . . Day 6
Proverbs 17:1 . . . . Day 6	II Thessalonians 3:10 . . . . Day 12
Proverbs 17:28 . . . . Day 18	James 1:23, 24, 25 . . . . Day 25
Proverbs 19:3 . . . . Day 11	James 4:7 . . . . Day 8
Proverbs 20:7 . . . . Day 23	I Peter 1:8-9 . . . . Day 30
Proverbs 22:15 . . . . Day 10	I Peter 2:2, 3 . . . . Day 20
Proverbs 25:20 . . . . Day 3	I Peter 2:25 . . . . Day 8
Proverbs 29:21 . . . . Day 4	I Peter 3:4 . . . . Day 6
Proverbs 31:10-31 . . . . Day 15	I Peter 3:15 . . . . Day 27
Jeremiah 23:23 . . . . Day 13	II Peter 3:9 . . . . Day 29

Made in United States
Orlando, FL
05 December 2022